Beamish is a museum which tells the story of the people of north-east England at two distinct points in their history – 1825 and 1913. In 1825 the region was rural and thinly populated. Our towns and cities, though well known, were only small centres of trading and administration. The wealth of underground coal in the area and the coming of the railways changed all that. Traditional industries – coal, lead, steel, chemicals, shipbuilding, heavy engineering, brewing – became world famous, and by 1913 had reached their peak. Their success changed the physical landscape, patterns of settlement, the tradition and ways of life of the people in the North East.

History never seems like history when you are living through it. Looking back it is possible to see shapes and patterns, to consider how things might have developed differently and to learn a great deal. Our today – yesterday's future – could have been better for this perspective, and our future could also be made better for it. This is the purpose of Beamish.

Beamish is not a traditional museum. Some buildings in the Beamish Valley, such as the Drift Mine, Home Farm and Pockerley Manor, were here already and have been restored. Most of the buildings, however, have been rescued from elsewhere in the North East, transported here and rebuilt. The Museum is a three-dimensional architectural jigsaw. All our buildings are filled with objects, furniture and machinery – real things from our extensive collections. We hope that the scholarship and detailed research don't show… but they're behind everything we do.

You will find no glass cases and very few labels and information boards. We believe they are intrusive. Within our buildings you will find people who are trained to talk to visitors and answer questions. The staff are proud of their heritage. You are under no compulsion to listen to them but the quality of your visit will be improved if you do. It is this personal interpretation of the site that distinguishes Beamish from other museums.

Li... peo... site; many come back the next day.

Study the map. All of our locations, transport routes, catering sites and toilet facilities are clearly marked. Plan your route carefully. Most visitors, seduced by the sight of trams, travel into the Town and work their way back by tram, bus or on foot to the car park, leaving Pockerley Manor and the Colliery Village to the last. If you do so on a busy day you will move with the crowd. The wait is shorter to go underground at the Drift Mine in the morning. Pockerley Manor always takes more time than visitors expect. We advise you to go to both of these areas earlier rather than later in your visit.

Remember that Beamish has a serious purpose. It is a museum and not a theme park. Our purpose is to educate and to enlighten you, and if you enjoy the process we will be doubly pleased.

Peter Lewis, Director

The early nineteenth century was a period of great potential and also of social turmoil. After the French Revolution, Britain had been at war with France: Nelson was dead, having won his famous battle at Trafalgar, and Napoleon, defeated at the Battle of Waterloo in 1815, had been exiled to St Helena. At home, the nation which George IV ruled was an unquiet one, with plots and rebellions throughout the realm.

Literature was flourishing – Jane Austen's major novels had recently been published, Sir Walter Scott was widely read, and children's bedside reading included Charles Lamb's *Tales from Shakespeare*. Great advances of invention and technology were being made… the last 20 years had seen the completion of the Grand Junction and Caledonian Canals, Macadam was advocating revolutionary methods of building roads, Davy's safety lamp was in use, Telford had built the Menai Bridge, and here in the North East the Stockton and Darlington Railway had opened. In 1810 George Stephenson had promised that he would do something to 'astonish all England'. By 1830 he would be regretting the 'shameful way the country is going to be cut up by Railways'!

There have been people living at Pockerley for over 1000 years. Now a farm and house, this is an ancient defensive site – evidence of a far from peaceful past. The Reivers, both Scots and English, once rampaged over this countryside. The Old House was built in approximately 1400. The newer manor house, with its large windows and red roof, dates from about 1720. The house, gardens and farm buildings are of a kind that typically would be owned by a yeoman farmer and landowner.

The south-facing terraces contain formal gardens, cultivated vegetable plots and orchards. All the plant, shrub and tree species found here were available in the 1820s. The contemporary lists published by William Falla's nurseries in Gateshead, which covered over 600 acres, have proved invaluable for our research. The surrounding woods and fields were once a fine example of a Georgian enclosure landscape. Gradually, by replanting hedges and by 'ridge and furrow' ploughing, that landscape will be restored.

Far left: *Packhorse and driver approaching Pockerley Manor*
Middle: *The formal gardens at Pockerley Manor*
Left: *Woodcut of a farmer's boy by Davison of Alnwick*

The manor house is shown as it was in the 1820s when a yeoman landowner, along with his family, servants and labourers, ran the surrounding farm estate.

The **back kitchen** has a peat fire. This is the room where clothes are washed, dishes cleaned, and food prepared.

Left: The Durham Ox, an etching by J. Whessel after J. Boultbee, Durham, 1802
Right: Clock dial by Beilby & Hawthorn of Newcastle upon Tyne, on a clock by Ralph Weston of Wolsingham, 1812

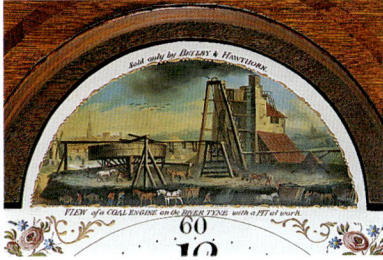

Note the large copper boiler and the marble slab. A plunger churn makes butter. The tools stored here are used for peat-cutting, pig-killing, sheep-clipping and net repairs.

The **pantry** on the north side of the house is well ventilated and painted with limewash to discourage flies and bugs. Salt fish, pheasants, rabbits and a turkey hang from hooks. Also stored here are soap, candles, sugar loaves, pickles, preserves, fresh vegetables and herbs.

The **kitchen** is the most important room in the house. The cooking range and bread oven are frequently in use. A large pine table with a sycamore top is both the main working area and the place where the extended family takes its meals. The kitchen furniture is mostly made of solid oak. The dresser holds pewter plates and Spode blue and white pottery. A very unusual oak long-case clock has a rare face with a painted colliery scene.

The **parlour** is the family's special room. It has elegant painted pine panelling and provincial country-style furniture, including an oak gate-leg table with mahogany cupboards and bureau. The paintings and engravings celebrate the family's interests in stock-breeding.

Note the portraits of Durham Shorthorns, the Northumberland Ox and Chestnut Arabian Stallion. This special room is heated by coal and has more expensive candles, made of beeswax rather than the more common tallow variety seen elsewhere.

Left: *Rodham Jug – Sunderland Ware*
Above: *The Pantry*

This is a back-and-front house rather than the upstairs/downstairs system of later Victorian houses. The servants live in the smaller, darker, north-facing rooms at the back of the house, the family in the sunnier front rooms.

The single servants would live in strictly segregated male and female rooms. Note the scant furnishings, lack of fires and absence of privacy. Married servants would 'live out'.

The **master bedroom** has a four-poster Georgian bed with chintz hangings and a fine hand-worked coverlet. Under the linen bedclothes are mattresses filled with flock and soft feathers. The shutters of the windows are original.

from pieces of old oak panelling, where sides of bacon and ham were hung and smoked. The shutter on the wall allows wood-smoke, usually from burning oak, from the kitchen range below, to seep into the loft.

Behind the house in the farmstead buildings are Georgian stables, home to the estate's Clydesdales, Cleveland Bays and Dales ponies. A pack-horse route passes through the farmyard.

The scrubbed wood floors were regularly limewashed to deter bugs and vermin. The mats and rugs are mostly oriental. Most of the prints and pictures in the bedroom relate to rural life but also include portraits of 'Capability' Brown and Master Lambton – the Red Boy. The hunting-horn on the chair beside the bed was used by the master of the house to wake up the servant-lads in order to feed the horses.

The **middle bedroom**, with its arsenic green wallpaper, contains a smaller four-poster bed. Underneath is stored a child's truckle bed.

The third bedroom is a **storage room**; it was common to have such a room in the nineteenth century. Large chests contain feed corn, meal and other grains. Hanging on the walls are stack nets and some man-traps. Woe betide any poachers who set foot upon the estate illegally. Behind the screen is the loft, made

Far left: The middle bedroom
***Middle:** Master bedroom*
***Left:** Early nineteenth-century engraving showing a poacher caught in a man-trap*
***Top:** The servant-lads' room*

The **Old House** dates from 1440 and formed the strong-house wing of an early manor. The undercroft has massive walls, five feet thick; valuables were kept here during border raids. By 1820, the rooms upstairs were let to farm labourers and miners' families as living-rooms and attic bedrooms.

Right: Candle-making in the Old House

Below: Chimney-crane and hearth in the Old House

In the valley-bottom, below the terraces of the house, runs Pockerley Waggonway. Horse-hauled waggonways had existed since the sixteenth century. It was in the North East that George Stephenson and his contemporaries developed the first steam-powered railways.

The Great Shed is based upon the lost buildings of Timothy Hackworth's works at Shildon, County Durham. Incorporated in the structure is original ironwork from George Stephenson's Forth Banks works at Newcastle upon Tyne. At the centre of these is Stephenson's industrial locomotive, one of five built for Hetton Colliery in 1822. This is reputedly the third oldest surviving railway engine in the world. Other displays include an engineman's shelter, engineer's office and items of early rolling stock.

From 1999, visitors may have the opportunity to experience steam-hauled travel in unsprung recreated carriages behind the working replica of George Stephenson's *Locomotion*. If finance materialises we hope to recreate a lost locomotive of 1815, the *Steam Elephant*. In time, other displays will include a horse-worked wooden waggonway extending to a gin-pit and limekiln above Pockerley crossroads. We also plan to develop the

Left: Wrought-iron weather-vane on the Great Shed, Pockerley Waggonway
Right: Sketch of Sir Humphrey Davy's lamp from Matthias Dunn's diary of 1816

forges, flint and water mills alongside Beamish Burn.

Note that this exhibit will open in stages during the lifetime of this guidebook. Check with staff for details.

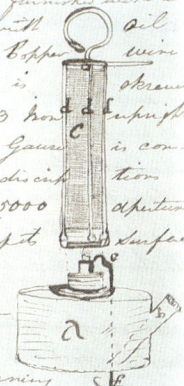

Main picture: *The replica of* Locomotion *below Pockerley*
Far left: *Hetton Colliery Locomotive of 1822, built by George Stephenson for the Hetton Colliery Railway*
Middle: *The* Steam Elephant: *the world's oldest painting of a locomotive*

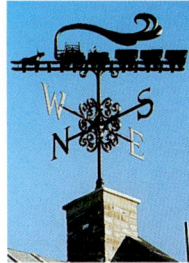

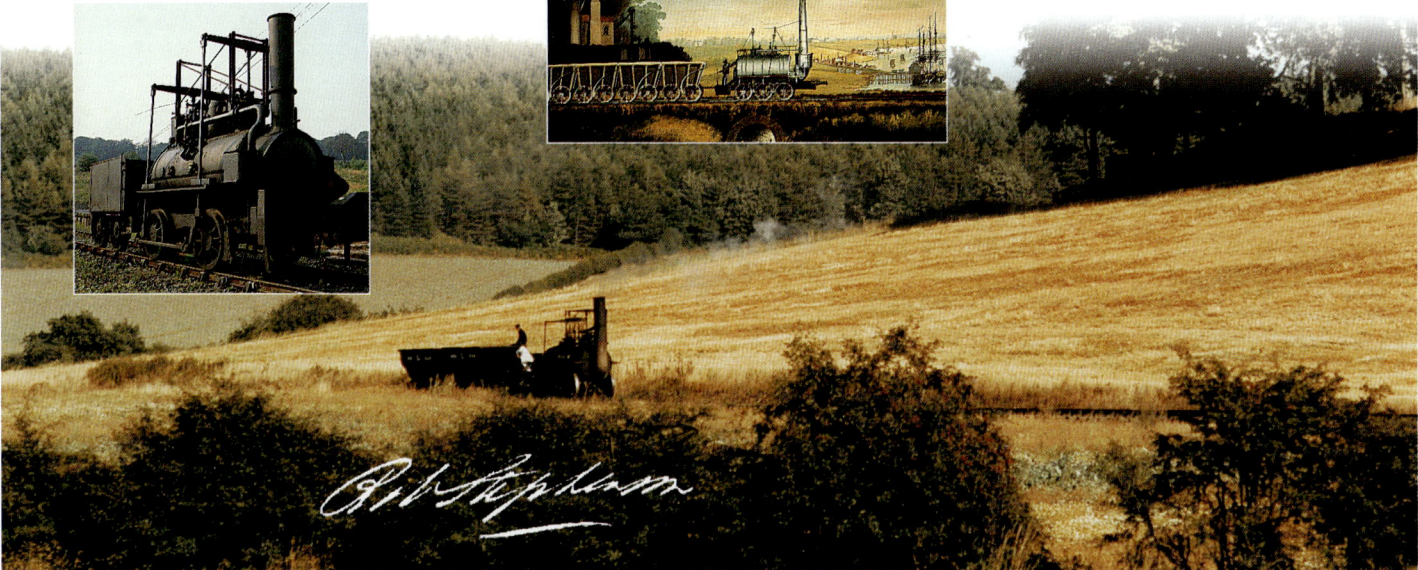

The first years of the twentieth century were momentous. The 60-year reign of Queen Victoria ended in 1901, to be followed by the relatively brief reign of Edward VII, and in 1910 George V came to the throne. The South African War ended, and the First World War was about to begin.

In America the Wright Brothers had flown the first aeroplane, and nearer home Blériot had flown the Channel. Campaigns were being fought over women's suffrage. Old-age pensions had been introduced, and a new Education Act had been passed. The Labour Party had won some seats in the two general elections won by Asquith's Liberal Party. Captain Scott had reached the South Pole, and the unsinkable *Titanic* had struck an iceberg in the Atlantic.

Coal, the 'black diamond', was once the life-blood of industry and a central part of life, particularly in this region. No recreation of the history of the North East would be complete without a colliery and the people who worked and lived in and around it.

The extraction and use of coal powered this region. At its peak in 1913, the Great Northern Coalfield employed nearly a quarter of a million men and boys, producing over 56 million tons of coal yearly from roughly 400 pits. Towns like Seaham Harbour, West

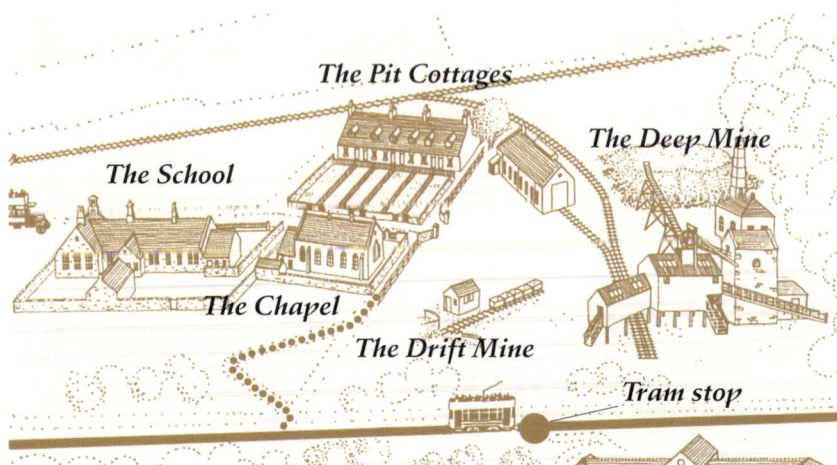

The Pit Cottages

The School

The Deep Mine

The Chapel

The Drift Mine

Tram stop

Hartlepool and Bedlington owed their very existence to coal.

Entrepreneurs like John Buddle, the 'King of the Coal Trade', made their fortunes. The Shaftos of Beamish Hall, relatives of the famous Bobby Shafto (he of the silver buckles), owned pits and also the ships that took coal from Newcastle to London and onwards to Scandinavia, Germany, the Low Countries and France.

Though in 1913 the North East produced a quarter of Britain's coal, the region's supremacy was coming under challenge from the coalfields of South Wales and Yorkshire, where seams were more easily accessible.

Today, as the twentieth century draws to its close, the coal industry has all but ceased to exist, but it changed the landscape, patterns of settlement, traditions and way of life of this region for ever.

Far left: *The pit cottages built between 1860 and 1865*
Main picture: *Pit cottage No. 4 – a poor household*
Top: *Pay-day in the Colliery Office*

The pit cottages from Francis Street, Hetton-le-Hole were built in the 1860s for pitmen and their families. Pits were often isolated, and the homes built near them became close-knit communities of mutually dependent families. Miners' wages were comparatively high, as the solid furniture and good furnishings found in the cottages show.

Far left: The kitchen of No. 3, the home of an Irish Catholic family
Bottom left: The front room of No. 3
Left: Sunderland Ware plaque

Methodist and Roman Catholic. No. 4 is sparser; a miner's widow and her eldest two sons are the only breadwinners for the family. Note the pitmen's gardens, the poultry and rabbit-runs and the inevitable pigeon crees.

Below: The front room of No. 2, home of an elderly Methodist couple
Below left: 'God in the Bottle' – a traditional symbolic depiction of the crucifixion

Five houses from the original 27 are shown. No. 1 is the colliery office, where miners collected their fortnightly wages. Nos. 2 and 3 are lived in by neighbours from different religious traditions –

In the colliery yard is the entrance to Mahogany Drift Mine. The origins of the name are a mystery. The mine, a tunnel (or 'drift') driven into the hillside, first opened in the 1850s and was worked intermittently during the nineteenth century. It was re-opened in 1921 to serve Beamish Chophill Colliery.

Visitors can walk into the first seam underground to see and feel what miners'

working conditions were like.

'Hewers' cut coal by hand or with compressed-air cutters. They worked an eight-hour shift in difficult, dark, wet conditions. 'Fillers' shovelled coal into tubs, which were then pushed by 'putters' to the main haulage road. Trains of tubs were then pulled to the surface by pit ponies, rope haulage or engines.

Above: Bait time in Mahogany Drift Mine
Far left: Pip and handler
Left: A Stanley miner wearing typical clothing. He is carrying a safety lamp and pick, and has bandy legs due to rickets

Coal was moved from the pit-head by railway. Most collieries developed their own systems, and in the North East some of these systems were very extensive, with lines connecting to the North Eastern Railway system for further distribution.

The engine shed is a recreation of one which once stood at Beamish No. 2 Pit. Locomotives on display may include No. 14 *Hawthorne Leslie* from the Lambton and Hetton Railway and *Malleable* No. 5 from the South Durham Iron and Steelworks. Earlier still are *Coffee Pot*, an 0-4-0 vertical powered locomotive from Stockton on Tees (1871), and *Lewin* 683 which once worked at Seaham Harbour. All around the Colliery are examples of typical north-eastern chaldron waggons.

The Colliery Village at Beamish is built around a recreation of a typical pit of the early 1900s.

A tall stone engine house and wheel dominates the

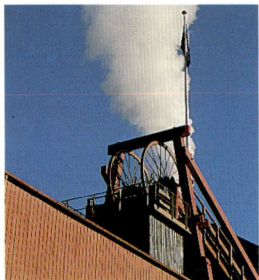

skyline. It was once Beamish Colliery Pit No. 2 - sometimes known as 'Chophill' - and contains a

working steam winder built in 1855 by J. & G. Joicey & Co. This winder is the unique survivor of a type once common in the region. To the rear of the winding house is a jack engine, used to lower heavy equipment down the shaft. It can also lower and raise cages when maintenance work is undertaken to the headstock.

Next to the engine house is a wooden heapstead building and screens brought here from Ravensworth Park Drift Mine, Gateshead. Here,

cages are drawn up from the shaft below. Tubs are pulled clear and the coal tipped on to screens for sorting and cleaning before being sent to the black chaldron waggons waiting below. Stone, dust and waste are pushed out over the gantry to the ever-growing spoil heap. Below the screens is the powerful sinking engine from Silksworth Colliery – used when shafts were being sunk or widened. At the edge of the wood, beyond the winding house, is a small powder house from Houghton Colliery, used to store explosives for use underground.

Mining was, and remains, a very dangerous occupation. Roof-falls, fires, explosions,

Above: *The steam-winder built by J. & G. Joicey & Co. of Newcastle upon Tyne, 1855*
Above left: *The Edward Medal, presented for outstanding bravery in mine rescues*
Far left, left: *Hewing coal at 'A' pit, Brancepeth Colliery, Willington*

suffocating gases and inrushes of water have all taken scores of lives. The effect of these disasters is brought home vividly by an entry in the East Stanley Junior Mixed School logbook: 'Many of our children have lost fathers or brothers. The intense grief is unbearable. So few were present that we did not mark the register.' On the afternoon of 16 February 1909 a massive blast had killed 168 men and boys in West Stanley Colliery.

Above: *Checking the weight of tubs*
Left: *The heapstead, screens and sidings*

Adults often romanticise school as 'the happiest days of their lives'. Children are more cynical, and for them the expression 'back to school' is not a joyful one. Yet education has always represented an escape route from hardship – a way of 'getting on'.

Beamish Board School once stood in nearby East Stanley. It was first opened in 1892 and when it closed, nearly a century later, three classrooms were rebuilt at Beamish. They would have accommodated up to 200 children.

At the turn of this century school attendance was compulsory; the school leaving age was 12 years. Bright pupils who reached basic levels in reading, writing and arithmetic often left school in order to support their families. Few went on to further education, though some undertook five-year apprenticeships as pupil teachers.

Board schools were built to last. They had high architectural standards which avoided expensive maintenance. They were light and airy, a necessary feature in an era of poor hygiene. The school day was hard: even the infants spent most of their days at their desks.

Many children from once notoriously tough areas like East Stanley started school as young as three years old; mothers with large families sent toddlers to school with their elder brothers or sisters so they could get on with their housework.

The purpose of education was to create law-abiding, useful citizens. Children were trained to 'know their place' and to 'show respect for their betters'. Learning was instilled by rote and repetition. Doing sums -

Top: *The school attendance board*
Left: *An educational wallchart on how to avoid tuberculosis*
Above: *Pupils of Sutton Primary School, Hull*
Above right: *Girls exercising with dumb-bells in the school-yard*
Right: *Typical Edwardian classroom scene*

pounds, shillings and pence - and chanting multiplication tables were daily rituals. As well as reading, writing and arithmetic, instruction was also given in geography, history, domestic science, needlework, music, religious knowledge, hygiene and exercise drill. Educational posters and charts illustrated a wide variety of topics. The importance of patriotism and the authority of the Empire (coloured red on the globe) were constantly emphasised.

Children first learnt to write on slates before progressing to dip-pens and exercise books, where they practised ornate copperplate writing. Discipline was hard, with the cane or leather tawse as the ultimate deterrents.

The punishment book recorded all misdemeanours.

Despite the best efforts of truant officers, children were often absent, especially in the spring or at harvest time. Illness was common: malnutrition and poor sanitation meant that diseases like typhoid, tuberculosis, diphtheria, measles, influenza and scarlatina were common. In 1913, antibiotics were as yet unknown.

In the playground children enjoyed their seasonal games of conkers, marbles, boolers and hopscotch. Each small locality had its own chants and rhymes, and games with ball and skipping-rope.

Above: *The Kindergarten in the Board School*
Left: *An Edwardian lesson*

Pit Hill Methodist Chapel was built in 1854 to serve the local mining and farming communities. Non-conformist Christianity, with its chapels rather than churches, flourished in the North East. Methodism, founded by John and Charles Wesley, had three main centres: London, Bristol and Newcastle upon Tyne. It encompassed several shades of opinion – Pit Hill represents the more respectable Wesleyan Methodists, but there were also Primitive Methodists, who were especially strong in mining communities; they were more radical and fiercely independent. Other denominations such as Baptists, Congregationalists, Presbyterians, Quakers and the Salvation Army were also well represented in the region.

The chapel fulfilled both the social and spiritual needs of its members. In addition to the services – three on Sundays and several more in midweek – there were women's meetings, Bible classes, temperance groups (or 'Rechabites'), choirs and Sunday schools. To cater for a growing membership, the chapel was enlarged in 1876 and again in 1904. Chapel folk supported home and foreign missions and served on local hospital and charity boards. At a time when opportunities for education were limited, the chapel trained its members, teaching them to keep minutes, conduct meetings, and balance accounts. These were skills people took with them into the Liberal and Labour parties and trade unionism.

Chapels were well-scrubbed, highly polished places: cleanliness was

Above: *Fundraising for the Primitive Methodists*

Below: Methodist Love
Feast Mug
Bottom: Harvest Festival

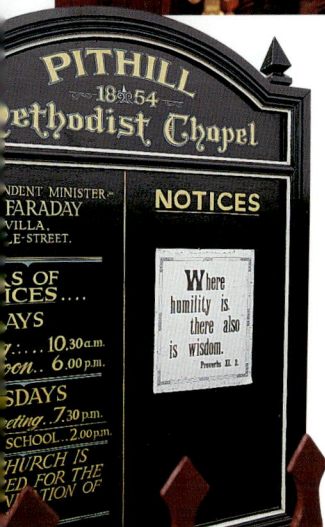

Wesleyan Methodist Church.

Quarterly Ticket of Membership.

SEPTEMBER, 1906.

Follow after peace with all men, and the
sanctification without which no man shall
see the Lord.—*Heb.* xii. 14 (R.V.)

Chris Arneson.

next to godliness. The usual church festivals were celebrated and the weeks of the Chapel Anniversary and the Sunday School Anniversary were also important, featuring special events, concerts, talks, and magic lantern shows.

An illustrated book, *Our Chapel,* is available from the Museum Shop.

PITHILL
1854
Methodist Chapel

DENT MINISTER
FARADAY
VILLA,
E-STREET.

NOTICES

S OF
ICES....
AYS
7.:.... 10.30 a.m.
on. 6.00 p.m.

SDAYS
eting..7.30 p.m.
SCHOOL..2.00 p.m.

HURCH IS
ED FOR THE
TION OF

Where
humility is
there also
is wisdom.
Proverbs XI. 2.

The Town represents a typical north-eastern market town of the years just before the First World War. The region's towns grew rapidly from the 1870s onwards, with some seeing considerable improvements in sanitation, water supply, street lighting and other amenities. The results of many of these changes can be seen in the Town.

At the west end of the Town is a Victorian park with ornamental flower beds and a bandstand originally from Saltwell Park in Gateshead. Brass band concerts are held here on some Sunday afternoons. Further along the street is the Co-operative store. The building, from Annfield Plain, dates from the 1870s. By 1913 shops and department stores had replaced most of the old

street markets from earlier times. The Beamish Motor and Cycle Works is next door and supplies everything from the latest model of car to gramophones and sewing machines. The Jubilee Confectioners and the Branch Newspaper Office are opposite, both serving the growing mass market. The Sun Inn, originally from Bishop Auckland, dates from the 1860s. The interior, although altered many times over the years, has been rebuilt much as it was originally, with a 'Bar' and a 'Select'. The Livery Stables just behind the pub are facing growing competition from the Garage.

The Town is dominated by the row of Georgian houses. Ravensworth Terrace, from Gateshead, was built between 1830 and 1845. These are family houses, built for aspiring professionals and

Map labels:

The Sun Inn
Brewery Stables
The Newspaper Office
The Sweet Shop
Ravensworth Terrace
The Bank
Tram stop
Park
The Garage
The Co-op and Tearoom

tradesmen. The gas and electric lighting and comfortable furnishings illustrate the growing sophistication of town life available to those who could afford it.

Right: *Consett water-fountain of 1878*

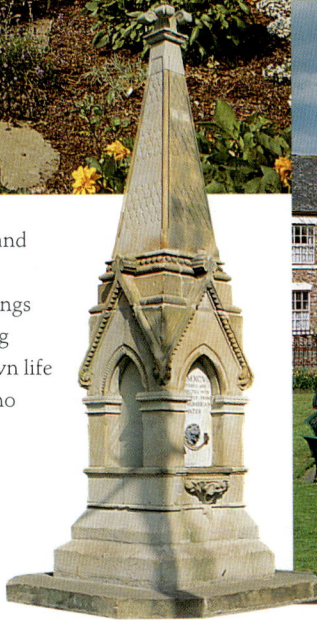

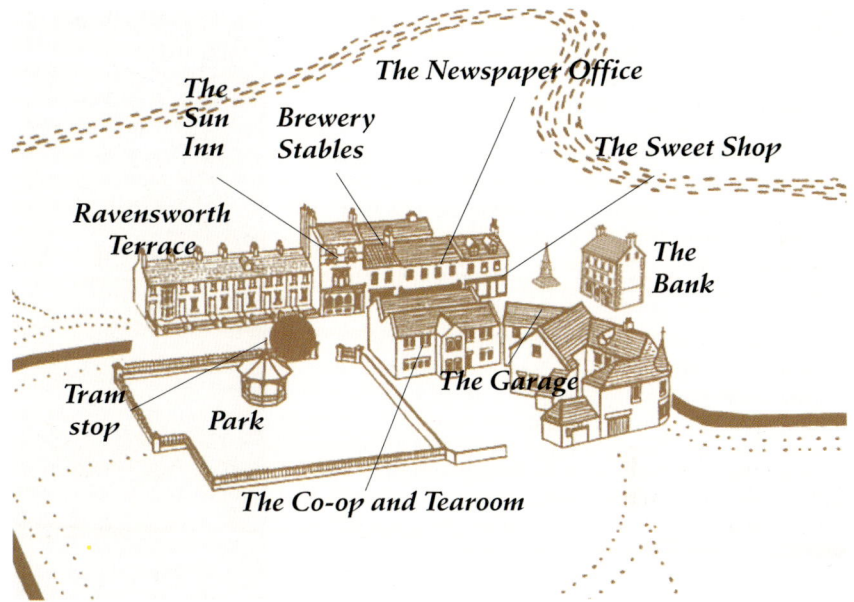

No. 2 Ravensworth Terrace represents the home of Miss Florence Smith, a teacher of singing, piano and elocution, who inherited this house and its contents from her parents and has made few changes to it. The house still has an old-fashioned feel, with furniture and furnishings from the earlier mid-Victorian period. Miss Smith's home is lit by oil lamps – not for her the gas or electricity of her near-neighbour the dentist.

The cluttered parlour, with its drapes and heavy curtains, is where Miss Smith teaches her pupils. She charges sixpence (less than 3p today) for a lesson. The furniture is of good quality walnut and there are some especially fine balloon-back chairs by Sopwith, the renowned cabinet-makers of Newcastle upon Tyne.

The kitchen is primitive by modern standards. The floor is laid with stone flags and cooking is done on the cast-iron kitchen range;

Above: *Maid of all work*
Left: *Kitchen in No. 2, Ravensworth Terrace*
Right: *Front room in No. 2*

no labour-saving devices here. The hall, stairs and landing have traditional grained paint work, skirtings and dados. The stained-glass window on the landing, typical of the period, shows an allegorical figure of a lady with a dove.

The main bedrooms are full of heavy mahogany furniture. Note the large four-poster bed with its embroidered quilt and coverings. There is no bathroom or water closet – each bedroom has its own washstand, and under each bed is the usual equipment. This house, unlike next door, has not yet been brought up to 1913 standards.

The Holborn Model VIII.

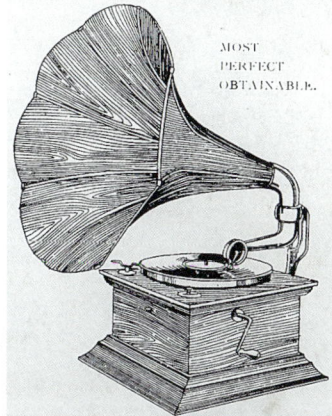

MOST PERFECT OBTAINABLE.

Cabinet—Best English manufactured Oak, finely polished, hinged top to Motor. Motor—New Patent worm gear, silent running, extra strong double spring, accurate speed indicator. 12 in. Turntable. Tone Arm—Finely adjusted with patent swivel, extra heavy and well tapered. Sound Box—The Famous "Crescendo." Horn—Dark Oak polished, new design Bell 22 in², length 26 in.

Price £3 15 0

filled with prints, books and toys. The bathroom and toilet contain a new-fangled Shanks bath, canopy shower, and a Doulton Patent Combination Flush Closet.

The master bedroom is dominated by a brass half-tester bed, covered by a traditional quilt. One large room in the attic accommodates the servants. Downstairs in the kitchen, new and old combine: the large black kitchen range remains, but there is also a new gas cooker, a knife-cleaner and

a forerunner of the vacuum cleaner. The drawing-room retains its original fireplace, glass cabinets and shutters and is furnished with reproduction Sheraton-style furniture.

Left & centre: The dentist's kitchen, showing the Glendinning-type range and the bathroom, with bath and canopy shower manufactured by Shanks & Co.
Below: The master bedroom, with its fine 'Italian' bedstead

I n 1913 there were still tooth-pullers operating from street markets. The profession of dentistry was relatively new and was often practised from home. At No. 3 Ravensworth Terrace the downstairs parlour is used as a waiting room, and upstairs are the surgery, recovery room and technician's workshop.

An upstairs corridor leads into No. 4, the dentist's family residence, elegantly furnished to the taste of 1913. The sunny front-facing nursery is

No. 5 Ravensworth Terrace contains the offices of J. & R.S. Watson, typical of many small-town solicitors of the early 1900s. Robert Spence Watson was a Quaker, with a legal practice in Newcastle upon Tyne. A radical liberal and pioneer of industrial arbitration, he became a national figure in politics and education.

The Principal's office is at the front of the house. On the partner's desk are documents tied with pink ribbon (or red tape perhaps?). The small standing desk was used by the solicitor when acting as a Registrar of Births, Marriages and Deaths. Also here is the book where duplicates of written letters were made on dampened tissue paper. Stacked around the walls are the named deed-boxes of prominent local families.

The office was old-fashioned even in 1913. Many solicitors were reluctant to install modern equipment like telephones, and some still preferred speaking tubes for internal communication. The general office, or clerks' office, is at the rear. It has a Dickensian feel, with high stools, gas lights and old engravings. Here the clerks would copy opinions, wills and file the firm's documents.

Above: *Robert Spence Watson*
Left: *At work in the clerks' office*
Right: *The Principal's office*

Mr J. S. Challoner & others

to

Mr. Henry Fawcus
and another.

Conveyance
of
freehold premises No. 14 Ravensworth Terrace
Gateshead in the County of Durham

The British have a great love of sugar, and Jubilee Confectioners panders to this affection with its enticing window displays, interior mahogany fittings, mirrors and bright lights. The glass jars are full of sugared almonds, aniseed balls, mints, pastilles and liquorice, as well as regional favourites like cinder toffee, black bullets and Poor Bens. Other local sweets included Horners' Dainty Dinah, Mermaid and Boy Blue Toffees.

In the factory behind the shop visitors can see the process of traditional sweet-making. The sugar is boiled in large copper pans, flavoured, coloured and cooled before being cut by rollers into a variety of shapes – stars, fishes, letters of the alphabet and many more. The equipment used and stored

Left: *Making cinder toffee in the sweet-works*
Below: *Advertisement for Fry's chocolate*

FRY'S MILK CHOCOLATE

MAKERS TO H M THE KING · 300 GOLD MEDALS &

2 FOR 2ᴰ

on the walls came from a confectionery works in Houghton-le-Spring and from Rowntree's at York.

The tremendous variety of sweets and chocolates is a modern phenomenon. In its infancy, chocolate was a drink which only the privileged few could afford, then recipes for combining sugar with cocoa created chocolate for eating. Improvements in mechanisation along with more reliable transport and distribution made it possible to develop nationwide brand names like Fry's, Terry's, Cadbury's and Rowntree's. It is an irony that companies founded by serious Quakers and chapel-goers should have provided such irresistible temptations.

Left: *A toffee hammer*

The Beamish Motor and Cycle Works is a typical town garage of the period before the First World War. Edwardian garages combined the skills of the blacksmith, wheelwright and coach builder and were housed in converted rather than purpose-built buildings with large workshops. Petrol was not supplied from pumps but in two-gallon cans.

The showroom contains new and second-hand cars and motor cycles. A variety of vehicles is shown, notably the unique Armstrong Whitworth limousine of 1908, made in Newcastle upon Tyne. On the walls can be seen a large display of enamel advertisements from the period.

In 1913 there was little standardisation of spare parts – most were made or remade to order in the workshop. Horns and lighting sets – gas, electric or acetylene – were supplied as extras. The Vulcaniser tyre-repair system is of particular interest. One of Henry Ford's Model T cars is shown under repair, as is an early local Daimler removal lorry. Garages of this size would also have hired out charabancs and acted as haulage contractors.

The replica car, a 1912 Armstrong Whitworth limousine, is regularly in use in the Museum, travelling between the Town and the Colliery Village. This Edwardian building fits the early requirements of the *Cycle and Motor Trade Review* which said in May 1908 that a garage should be 'a shop for the supply of the motorist's numerous accessories… an engineering works… and care and shelter for the complete car.'

Top left: Armstrong Whitworth radiator badge
Above: *North Eastern Automobile Association radiator badge*
Left: *Armstrong Whitworth 30/50 limousine of 1908*
Right: *The Garage showroom, with its Model T Ford*

Across the Street from the Co-op, the news headlines for 1913 are prominently displayed outside the branch office of a local newspaper. Newspapers were printed elsewhere on high-speed presses and distributed to branch offices to be sold over the counter in newsagents and by street-sellers, but the office was more than just a distribution point. Upstairs a jobbing printer produced posters, business cards, advertising material and private and commercial stationery for local customers. For short runs the Arab Platen Press was used, with more extensive orders and posters printed on the fast semi-automatic Wharfedale Press. At the rear of the print shop stands the magnificently ornamented early Victorian Columbia Press, easily identifiable by its eagle. Downstairs the shop stocks a range of specially selected cards, prints and copies of

TOW LAW LOCAL BOARD.

NOTICE.

Any person found depositing any Timber, Stone, Iron, Dung, Manure, Slops, or any other matter in the Channels or Street Traps, or upon the Streets or Highways within the Board District, will be prosecuted.

By order of the Board,
W. GARRAWAY, Inspector.
J. HILLARY, Surveyor.

Myles Taylor, Gas Printing Works, Hope Street, Crook.

Main picture: *The Columbia press in use*
Left: *The downstairs counter in the Newspaper Office*

Edwardian stationery. Look out for writing materials bearing the familiar household names of Reeves, Rowney, Watermans and Conway-Stewart.

In the Town a fine, four-storeyed branch of Barclays Bank is under construction, assembled from old bricks and quoins saved from Park House, Gateshead. The 'Swedish Imperial Red' granite frontage is typical of banks of this period. Strongrooms have been installed below.

Barclay & Company were formed in 1896 by an amalgamation of some 20 private banks, including three large north-eastern banks: Backhouse & Co., Woods & Co. and J.W. Pease & Co.

Above: *Barclay & Co.'s Bank, Beamish*
Left: *Bank in Barnard Castle*

The Co-operative movement revolutionised the lives of working-class people. Firstly, it gave them more control over the way they shopped for basic goods, but it also did much more, sending its own MPs to Westminster, encouraging women's suffrage and providing reading-rooms as well as venues for meetings, lectures and social functions.

The Co-op had its own factories which produced everything from sheets to soap and furniture, and many of these goods were sold in their stores. The hardware department sold mangles, possers, Pelaw Polish, paints, pots and pans, candlesticks, chamber pots, and furniture. Miners'

Main picture: Co-op Hardware counter
Centre: Co-op delivery bicycle

lamps, picks and shovels were also on sale; in those days pitmen had to provide their own gear.

The drapery department stocked dress and furnishing fabrics, haberdashery, a range of

buttons, hooks, feathers, crochet and lace materials. In labelled drawers and boxes were collars, hats, shoes, gloves, bags and purses. More discreetly displayed were corsets, camisoles and baby clothing. Hessian (or 'harn') for mat-making was available by the yard. Workmen's clothing, like the miners' traditional short trousers – 'pit-hoggers' – were also for sale.

Above the heads of customers roll the hollow balls of the Lamson-Paragon Cash System. The main cashier recorded each transaction in the ledger, totalling the purchases that would earn the all-important quarterly dividend, a forerunner of today's supermarket loyalty cards. Divi-day was a vital event for local housewives. When times were good, the dividend could be over four shillings in the pound – a rebate of 20%.

Co-op prices were rarely the cheapest, but the goods were reliable and the dividend was very welcome. Also important was the stability provided by the Co-operative Insurance Society's policies. 'Everything from the cradle to the grave' was the Co-op boast until, burdened by paperwork and bad management, it was overtaken by competitors.

Below: Check cloth was used to make pitmen's 'hoggers'

The first Co-operative store was a grocer's. The provision of high-quality, unadulterated food was of great importance in nineteenth-century Britain.

The Co-op was a major owner of dairy farmland in Northumberland and also owned bacon factories in Denmark and Ireland. Tea was imported from its own plantations. Most goods were weighed, measured and packed by hand. Note the lentils, split peas and sugar, all in colour-coded paper bags. Butter was cut and patted into shape from large casks, bacon sliced to the thickness requested by customers and coffee ground by hand. Biscuits were sold loose as were, when requested, cigarettes. Large orders were wrapped

in brown paper and string, while smaller items like sweets were served in hand-twisted paper cones. Chairs were provided for waiting customers.

Branded goods in cans were starting to appear: Colmans and Skipper Sardines are evident on the shelves. There was some fresh fruit and vegetables, but most purchases were preserved and shopping was done on a daily basis – little and often. The large ornate till registered total sales up to nineteen shillings and elevenpence, three farthings (less than £1 in modern currency). Do not imagine that food was cheap: in relation to average wages, food was more expensive for the average family in 1913 than it is today.

Left: Placing an order in the grocery department
Right: The bar in the Sun Inn
Above right: A drawing with a message of temperance entitled 'Twixt Drink and Duty, from The British Workman, *1895*

The Sun Inn is a typical pub of the period. The front bar is strictly a male preserve; note the sporting trophies, especially the much-loved whippet in a case. Women were allowed – albeit with some loss of reputation – into the Select Room at the back. Draft beers are still served here, though unfortunately not at period prices.

Through the adjoining arch is the brewery yard with its open cart and dray shed. The stables have an adjoining tack-room containing a gleaming array of harness and trophies.

Railways were pioneered in north-east England and spread rapidly throughout the world. Early railway history is shown at Pockerley Waggonway (see page 9).

Adjacent to the Town, Beamish Station recreates a typical branch line country station of the early twentieth century. The passenger building dates from 1867 and came from Rowley near Consett.

Winter weather was often a problem on the exposed lines of Northumberland, Durham and North Yorkshire. One train was recorded as being snowbound at Rowley for three days.

Other railway artefacts have been gathered from elsewhere in the region. The wrought-iron footbridge nearest to the Town came from Howden le Wear; the signal-box is from Carr House East, Consett. The cast-iron footbridge from Dunston

Staithes links the station with a Goods Warehouse and Office from Alnwick. Of particular interest are the coal and lime 'cells' from West Boldon built in 1834 for the Stanhope and Tyne Railway. Near the yard gates are a weighbridge from

Left: A snowbound locomotive and relief engine at Rowley station, January 1910
Above: Interior of the signal-box
Right: Beamish Station looking east

Waskerley and a coal
merchant's office from
Hexham. Within the
station area are a variety of
locos and freight and coal
waggons.

*Above: NER clock by Reid &
Sons of Newcastle upon Tyne*
*Below: NER platelayers'
warning horn*

Agriculture was, and is, an important industry in this region. The North East pioneered new ideas in livestock breeding. The world's first pedigree herdbook recording Shorthorn Cattle dates back to 1822.

The Beamish Valley was once full of farms and pits. Home Farm, managed by the landowner's bailiff, was a model of good practice for tenants on the estate. The farmhouse is over 250 years old, and before its adaptation was probably two cottages.

The heart of the farm kitchen is a large range by Moffat of Gateshead and a long communal table where both the family and the farm labourers were fed. Traditional cheeses are made and sold in the dairy throughout the summer. Regional cheeses are also available in the museum shop.

The external layout of Home Farm has changed little since the 1780s. A Gin-Gan, or horse engine, was added to power the threshing machine before it was itself superseded by a steam thresher. The tall chimney is typical of many north-eastern farmsteads.

Far left: Home Farm Forge
Left: Making oat cakes in the kitchen at Home Farm
Below: Threshing day at Low Waskerley Farm, Shotley Field

Other buildings include a combined pigsty (ground floor) and hen-house (first floor). The pigs provided both warmth and protection from predators for the hens.

Across the road, beside the duckpond, stands the bull hemmel and a corrugated-iron cattle shelter, which was one of the first of its kind when exhibited at the Royal Show in 1908.

Beamish keeps as many animals as it employs people. Like their human counterparts, the animals help us to interpret the past. We show traditional breeds, some now rare, in period settings. There are no fixed locations where animals are viewed; we are farmers, not zoo-keepers. Animals will be found in fields around the Museum or in pens and buildings. Our stock is cared for using modern methods by specialist trained staff under the guidance of the Museum's veterinary advisor. However tempted you may be please do not

Left: *Making cheese in Home Farm*
Right: *Prince and Sensation in the Fold Yard at Home Farm*
Bottom: *Saddleback pigs*

feed any of our animals, especially the horses. Visitors should also note that if you start to feed geese or ducks they can be very demanding… you have been warned !

Animal breeds on view include Teeswater and Cheviot Sheep, Shorthorn Cattle (descendants of the famous Durham Ox), Saddleback pigs, working horses, Dales ponies, Cleveland Bays and a wide range of geese, ducks and farmyard poultry.

Until long after the First World War, when petrol vehicles came into general use, deliveries were made using horse-drawn vehicles. Examples in one of two charabancs. The *Happy Days* charabanc was probably built by Tom Marston of Birmingham and may have started its working life at Morecambe carrying visitors along the promenade. The *Maxim* was built by Holland & Holland of London, a famous firm of carriage-builders, for Vaux Breweries of Sunderland. Horses also provided much of the pulling power on the land. Heavy horses can be seen hard at work cultivating the fields around the Museum.

Left: *A hay-cart and workers at rest after hay-gathering*
Far left: *The* Maxim *Charabanc*
Below: *The* Happy Days *Charabanc*

from the Museum's collections can be seen at work in the Town and Colliery Village. The Town stables are behind the Sun Inn and Print Shop. Here carriages and traps would have been available for hire. The Angus Rali Trap is a rare survivor from an important north-eastern maker.

During the summer, visitors can travel from the Town to Pockerley Bottom

By the end of the nineteenth century the expanding towns and cities of the region needed a cheap and efficient transport system. At first horse-drawn buses were used and then, briefly, horse-drawn trams. Experiments were also made with steam trams. However, in the late 1890s electric trams replaced both. The Beamish tramway fulfils a dual function: it provides a transport system and also gives visitors a period tram-riding experience.

The Beamish fleet consists of six restored trams. Blackpool 31 was built in 1901 and was in service there until 1984; it has been working at Beamish since 1987. Sheffield 264 dates from 1907 and operated until 1956. Tram 196 is a foreigner, originating from Oporto. Built to a pre-World War One

Left: Mann Steam Tractor of 1928, designed for direct traction and ploughing
Bottom left: *Replica 30/50 lift top limousine* **Below:** *Tram 114 - a 1901 A-class tram*

design, it has been painted in the Gateshead livery. Sheffield 513 was built in 1952 and represents the apogee of traditional British tram car design.

Gateshead 10, one of two local trams in the Beamish fleet, was built in 1925. It remained in local service until 1951, and after restoration it entered service at Beamish in 1973. Tram 114 is the latest addition to the fleet. It was built in 1901 for the opening of Newcastle's Electric Tramway. In 1940 it was sold to Sheffield. After a brief spell as a chicken

shed, 114 came home to Beamish in 1987 and entered service in 1996. The Museum is now working to restore Sunderland 16 - one of the city's first electric trams.

A replica bus runs between the Town and Colliery Village. It is a copy of a type which operated from the tram terminal at Low Fell to Chester le Street. By late 1913 the now Northern General Transport Co. Ltd. – a subsidiary of Gateshead Tramways – owned 27 buses, 17 of which were

Left: J2503 replica bus

Daimler CC double-deckers, the last to arrive being J2503, a replica of which now runs at Beamish.

As well as our daily activities, Beamish hosts a wide selection of special one-day events, exhibitions and demonstrations. Details of these can be found in the local media and on the Events Boards around the Museum.